DEDICATION

This is written in love and admiration of my mom and dad. Your conversations, life experience and desire to prioritize family are the best gifts to rearing a child, grooming a man and developing a responsible adult. You continue to make me proud. It is my hope, I provide you with the same feeling.

Also, I want to dedicate this book to my family. I'm thankful that we acknowledge, assist, build, celebrate, consult and encourage each other to dream, make the effort, persevere and to simply be our best... individually and as a unit. You are my blessing and my greatest gifts!

THE BLACK FAMILY GUIDE TO STOCKS

SIMPLE STRATEGIES FOR INVESTING AND BUILDING WEALTH

Ed Atkins

The Black Family Guide to Stocks
Simple Strategies for Investing and Building Wealth

ISBN: 978-1-965319-67-3
LCCN: 2026911043

Book Cover by Andres Rivas-Cruz
Editing by Mon Trice and Judy Carney

www.PurposePublishing.com
13194 US Hwy 301 S #417
Riverview, FL 33578

PREFACE

The journey of writing this book began with a simple but profound realization: financial literacy is one of the most valuable skills to personally own and pass on to the next generation. It is one of my best memories of my father. Starting at age 7, my father would have conversations with me that started with the words, *"If something happens to me...."* and it would end with, *".... and take care of your mother."* This conversation he would repeat almost annually till he took his last breath.

Since his passing, the responsibility to have these conversations with my own family has amplified. When my family was young, we were so busy establishing a strategic personalized plan that included education, exploration, fun and goal achievement. We didn't spend a lot of time chatting about financial matters except when we discussed the monthly allowance, the purpose and requirement of the allowance (pay for your fun activities, save for when you have a real need and tithe). Unfortunately, we didn't discuss wealth building... building with purpose. I believe it is important that... I teach them to fish.... equip them with the knowledge and tools to confidently navigate their own financial journey. That's where the idea for this book, The Black Family Guide to Stocks: Simple Strategies for Investing and Building Wealth, was born.

Investing can feel overwhelming, even intimidating, especially for those new to the stock market. There's an abundance of terms, strategies, and metrics that can easily confuse you. Through the need to start having these conversations with our family, I realized how important it was to break down these concepts into simple, actionable lessons—something approachable yet comprehensive enough to serve as a foundation for smart investing and better living.

This book is more than an educational resource; it's a reflection of my commitment to our family's well-being. It's a guide written with love and purpose—to spark conversations, encourage questions, and inspire confidence in making informed financial decisions. Each chapter was carefully designed to provide clear explanations, practical examples, and interactive exercises that make learning about stocks / investing engaging and relatable.

As you read this book, you will notice that the examples and scenarios are intentionally family-oriented. That's because investing is not just about numbers or profits; it's about creating opportunities and building a legacy. Whether it's saving for college, planning for retirement, or simply understanding how to grow your wealth over time, the principles outlined here are meant to empower our family—and anyone who picks up this book—to take charge of their financial future.

Black families, this book is for you. I hope it becomes a resource you return to, a tool you rely on, and a starting point for deeper conversations about financial literacy and wealth-building. May it inspire you to dream, think big, act wisely, and always strive for growth—not just in investments, but in life.

Let's embark on this journey together and learn how to make the most of the opportunities the stock market offers. The future is bright, and it's ours / yours to build.

Let's build a legacy!

DISCLAIMER

This book, **The Black Family Guide to Stocks**: Simple Strategies for Investing and Building Wealth, is intended for educational and informational purposes only. The content presented herein reflects my personal research, understanding, and experiences with investing. It is designed to provide a foundational overview of the stock market and to encourage thoughtful discussions about financial literacy within my family and among readers.

I want to emphasize that I am not a certified financial planner, stockbroker, or licensed investment advisor. While I have taken great care to ensure the accuracy and relevance of the information provided, it should not be considered professional financial advice. Every individual's financial situation is unique, and investment decisions should be made based on personal circumstances, goals, and risk tolerance. Readers are encouraged to consult with a qualified financial professional before making any investment decisions.

This book is written from the perspective of a father who deeply cares about his family's financial well-being and who seeks to empower others to build confidence in their financial journeys. It is not intended to replace professional advice or to serve as a comprehensive investment guide.

By using this book, you acknowledge and agree that the author is not liable for any financial outcomes resulting from the use of the information provided. Investing in the stock market involves risk, including the potential loss of principal, and past performance is not indicative of future results.

Thank you for allowing me to share this resource with you. My hope is that it inspires meaningful conversations and helps you take the first steps toward achieving your financial goals with clarity and confidence.

TABLE OF CONTENTS

INTRODUCTION

Investing in the stock market is often perceived as complex, intimidating, and reserved for financial experts. However, the truth is that anyone can participate in the stock market, build wealth, and achieve financial goals with the right knowledge and tools. This book, The Black Family Guide to Stocks: Simple Strategies for Investing and Building Wealth, was created with a clear and simple purpose: to provide my family—my wife and our three kid-ults (my wife's affectionate term for our young adult children) — with a foundational understanding of stocks and investing.

Whether you are looking to save for a big purchase, prepare for retirement, or simply grow your financial literacy, the stock market offers opportunities to build wealth. However, understanding the basics is crucial to making informed decisions and avoiding common pitfalls. This guide aims to break down the complexities of investing into easily digestible lessons that anyone, regardless of race, age or financial background, can understand and apply.

This book is designed not only as a resource for education but also as a conversation starter for our family. It's an opportunity to sit together, discuss financial goals, and learn practical strategies to achieve them. Each chapter builds on fundamental concepts, introduces key metrics and strategies, and provides real-world examples to connect theory to practice. The quizzes and interactive exercises included in this book are there to solidify your understanding and make the learning process engaging.

Here is what you can expect from this guide:

- **Foundational Knowledge**: Learn what stocks are, how the stock market operates, and why investing is a powerful tool for wealth creation.

- **Practical Strategies**: Understand key financial metrics, investment instruments, and strategies to grow your portfolio.
- **Real-World Applications**: Explore examples that bring abstract concepts to life and show how they apply to everyday investment decisions.
- **Interactive Learning**: Participate in exercises that encourage hands -on learning and foster discussions about money and investing.

My hope is that this book becomes a valuable resource for your journey into the world of investing. More importantly, I hope it sparks meaningful discussions about financial literacy and empowers each of us to make confident, informed decisions about our money. By learning together, we can build a strong foundation for long-term financial success and create a legacy of smart investing for generations to come – **legacy wealth building.**

So, let's start this journey together. Let's demystify the stock market, learn its language and unlock its potential to secure our financial futures.

CHAPTER 1

WHAT IS A STOCK?

Definition of a Stock

A stock represents ownership or equity in a company. When you purchase a stock, you become a shareholder and own a small part of the company. Each share you own entitles you to a portion of the company's earnings and assets.

What is a stock ticker symbol?

- A stock ticker symbol, also known as a stock symbol or ticker, is a unique combination of letters or numbers that identifies a company's publicly traded shares on a stock exchange.
- Ticker symbols are often one to five letters long and can be abbreviations of a company's name or related to the company in some way.
- For example, Apple's ticker symbol is AAPL, Exxon's is XOM, and Coca-Cola's is KO. Airbnb's ticker symbol is ABNB, and Petco's is WOOF.

Why Companies Issue Stocks

Companies issue stocks to raise money for their operations, growth, or projects. This process is known as an Initial Public Offering (IPO), where the company sells shares to the public for the first time.

Example: Imagine a company that makes electric scooters. To build a larger factory, they might issue stocks to raise funds. Investors buy shares, providing the company with capital to build a larger factory to support the potential of the company's growth, revenue and hopefully profits.

How Stocks Work in the Economy

Stocks are a crucial part of the global financial system. They:

- **Help Companies Grow:** Companies use the funds from selling stocks to expand their operations.
- **Enable Investors to Build Wealth:** Investors buy stocks hoping they will increase in value or pay dividends.
- **Reflect Economic Health:** Stock prices often move based on the broader economy.

Key Concept

When you own a stock, you are a part-owner of the company. This ownership sometimes gives you the right to:

- **Capital gains:** When the value of a stock increases above its original purchase price, the owner makes a capital gain. For example, if a stock is purchased for $50 and sold for $75, the owner makes a $25 capital gain
- **Voting Rights:** Stock owners typically can vote on important company decisions during annual shareholder meetings.
- **Dividends:** Companies may distribute a portion of their profits to shareholders in the form of dividends. Dividend distribution is considered passive income for the owner of the stock.

What is Passive Income? Passive income refers to earnings generated with minimal active effort after initial work or investment is complete.

Even though owning stock has great wealth building advantages, there are some disadvantages for you to know:

- **Volatile prices**: Stock prices can be risky and volatile, rising and falling quickly. These price changes are often related to company policies, which investors can't influence
- **Shares can lose value**: Shares can lose value if the company has financial problems or makes poor decisions.

Real-World Example: The Pizza Shop

Imagine you own a successful neighborhood pizza shop. Your pizzas are so popular that customers line up around the block every weekend. You've been running this shop for years, and now you're ready to grow your business by opening new locations, buying better equipment, or expanding your delivery services.

But there's one problem: you don't have enough money to fund this expansion on your own.

To raise the money you need, you decide to sell **shares** of your business.

Step 1: Dividing the Business into Shares

- You divide your pizza shop into 1,000 "shares," each representing a small portion of ownership in the business.
- As the owner, you decide to keep 600 shares for yourself and sell 400 shares to investors.

Step 2: Valuing the Shares

- You calculate that your pizza shop is worth $100,000 based on your profits and growth potential.
- Each share is valued at $100 ($100,000 ÷ 1,000 shares).

Step 3: Selling Shares to Investors

- You offer the 400 shares to local investors, raising \$40,000 (400 shares × \$100 per share).
- These investors now become **shareholders** and own 40% of your pizza shop (400 out of 1,000 shares).

Step 4: Using the Money

You use the \$40,000 to buy a new pizza oven, hire more staff, and open a second location.

Step 5: The Value of the Shares

- As your business grows, profits increase, and more customers flock to your new locations.
- The value of each share rises to \$150. If a shareholder decides to sell their shares, they can now make a **capital gain** of \$50 per share (\$150 - \$100).

Step 6: Dividends

If your business generates enough profit, you may decide to pay **dividends** to your shareholders. For example, you could distribute \$10 per share as a thank-you for their investment.

Quick Quiz

Chapter 1: What is a Stock?

1. Definition: What does owning a stock represent?

   A. Ownership in a company

   B. A loan to a company

   C. A product offered by the company

   D. A company's revenue source

2. Real-World Application: If you own 100 shares of a company that issues $5 per share as a dividend, how much passive income do you earn annually?

   A. $50

   B. $500

   C. $1,000

   D. $2,000

3. Stock Ticker Symbols: Which of the following is an example of a stock ticker symbol?

   A. APPL for Apple

   B. KO for Coca-Cola

   C. AMZ for Amazon

   D. WASH for Washing Machines

CHAPTER 2

THE STOCK MARKET

What is a Stock Market?

The stock market is a marketplace where investors buy and sell stocks and other securities. It provides a platform for companies to raise capital and for investors to trade ownership in businesses.

- **Key Function**: Facilitates the exchange of stocks between buyers and sellers at an agreed price.
- **Why It Matters**: The stock market is crucial for economic growth because it allows companies to access funding for expansion while giving investors opportunities to build wealth.

What is a Stock Exchange?

A stock exchange is a part of the stock market where the actual trading happens. Think of it as the "store" where stocks are bought and sold.

Physical or Electronic Platforms:

- The **New York Stock Exchange (NYSE)** is a physical exchange with a trading floor.
- The **NASDAQ** operates entirely electronically.

Key Role: Ensures transparency, fairness, and efficient price discovery for traded securities.

How Stock Prices Are Determined

Stock prices are not set by companies or stock exchanges. Instead, they are influenced by supply and demand in the market.

Example:

- If many investors want to buy shares of a company (high demand), the stock price goes up.
- If many investors want to sell shares (high supply), the stock price goes down.

Factors that affect stock prices:

- **Company Performance**: Strong earnings reports can increase demand for a stock.
- **Market Sentiment**: News and investor confidence can drive prices up or down.
- **Economic Indicators**: Interest rates, inflation, and GDP growth affect overall market performance.

Market Participants

The stock market includes various types of participants:

- **Retail Investors**: Individuals like you and me who buy and sell stocks for personal goals (e.g., saving for retirement, wealth & legacy building).
- **Institutional Investors**: Large entities like mutual funds, pension funds, and hedge funds that trade large volumes of stocks.
- **Market Makers**: Professionals or firms that ensure there's enough liquidity in the market by buying and selling stocks to meet demand.

What is an Index?

A stock market index is a measurement of the performance of a group of stocks. It helps investors track the overall market or specific sectors.

Top Three U.S. Indexes

- **S&P 500**: Tracks 500 of the largest companies in the U.S. It's often used as a benchmark for the overall market.
- **Dow Jones Industrial Average (DJIA)**: Tracks 30 large, well-established companies like Apple, Coca-Cola, and Boeing.
- **NASDAQ Composite**: Focuses on tech-heavy stocks like Microsoft, Amazon, and Tesla.

Why Indexes Matter

Indexes give investors a snapshot of market trends and help them make investment decisions (buy, sell or hold) and compare the performance of their portfolios.

 **How to Participate in the Stock Market**

Participating in the stock market involves opening a brokerage account, funding it, and buying or selling stocks. Below is a step-by-step guide:

Step 1: Understanding Brokerage Accounts

A brokerage account is a type of account that allows you to buy and sell stocks, ETFs, mutual funds, and other securities. There are two main types of brokers:

Full-Service Brokers:

- Offer personalized investment advice, research, and financial planning.
- Ideal for investors who want guidance but come with higher fees.

- Examples: Merrill Lynch, Morgan Stanley.

Online Brokers:

- Allow you to trade stocks on your own with user-friendly platforms.
- Lower fees compared to full-service brokers.
- Examples: Robinhood, Fidelity, Charles Schwab.

Step 2: Choosing a Broker

When selecting a broker, consider the following factors:

- **Fees**: Look for brokers with low or no trading commissions.
- **Platform Usability**: Choose a platform that is easy to navigate.
- **Educational Resources**: Some brokers offer tutorials and market analysis for beginners.

Account Types:

- Individual Taxable Accounts: Suitable for regular trading.
- Retirement Accounts: Such as IRAs (Individual Retirement Accounts) that offer tax advantages.

Step 3: Opening Your Account

Opening a brokerage account is a straightforward process:

- Visit the broker's website or app and start the account setup.
- Provide personal information, such as your name, address, and Social Security number.
- Answer questions about your financial goals and risk tolerance.

- Link your bank account to transfer funds into the brokerage account.

Step 4: Funding Your Account

- Deposit money into your brokerage account to begin investing.
- Many brokers allow you to start with a small amount, sometimes as low as $1.

Types of Deposits:

- Bank transfer (ACH).
- Wire transfer.
- Paper check or mobile deposit in some cases.

Step 5: Researching Stocks

Before buying a stock, research its potential for growth and risk. Focus on these tools and resources:

- **Stock Screeners**: Filter stocks based on criteria like price, P/E ratio, and market cap. Examples include Yahoo Finance and Morningstar.
- **Company Reports**: Read the company's quarterly earnings reports and annual filings (e.g., 10-K).
- **News and Analysis**: Follow reputable sources like Bloomberg, CNBC, or the Wall Street Journal.

Step 6: Placing Your First Trade

Once you've chosen a stock, you can place a trade through your brokerage account.

Decide the Order Type:

- **Market Order:** Buy or sell the stock immediately at the current market price.
- **Limit Order:** Set a specific price at which you want to buy or sell the stock.
- **Stop Order:** Automatically buy or sell when the stock reaches a certain price.

Example Trade:

You decide to buy 10 shares of Company XYZ at $50 each. If you place a market order, the total cost will be $500 (plus any fees).

Step 7: Monitoring Your Portfolio

After purchasing stocks, keep an eye on their performance:

- **Tracking Tools:** Use portfolio trackers available on your brokerage platform.
- **Key Metrics to Monitor:**
    - Current stock price vs. purchase price.
    - Dividend payments (if applicable).
    - Overall portfolio growth.

Step 8: Knowing When to Buy or Sell

Making smart investment decisions requires knowing when to hold, buy more, or sell:

- **Buy More:** When a stock shows consistent growth or is undervalued compared to its peers.
- **Hold:** If the stock is performing well and aligns with your long-term goals.

- **Sell**: When the stock has reached your target price or when market conditions change significantly.

Tips for Beginners

- **Start Small**: Invest an amount you're comfortable losing, as the stock market carries risks.
- **Diversify**: Avoid putting all your money into one stock; spread it across sectors or use ETFs for diversification.
- **Stay Informed**: Regularly educate yourself about market trends and economic factors.
- **Use Virtual Trading**: Practice trading without real money through simulators like the Investopedia Stock Simulator.

Real-World Example: The Impact of News on Stock Prices

Imagine a company named GreenDrive, which manufactures electric vehicles (EVs). GreenDrive is publicly traded, and its stock is listed on the NASDAQ under the ticker symbol GDV. Here's how different types of news can impact GreenDrive's stock price:

Positive News: A Breakthrough Product Launch

GreenDrive announces a revolutionary new EV battery that doubles the driving range compared to competitors. This breakthrough excites both consumers and investors because it positions GreenDrive as a leader in the EV market.

Investor Reaction:

- Many investors believe this innovation will lead to higher sales and profits for GreenDrive.

- Demand for GreenDrive's stock increases as more people want to buy shares to benefit from the company's potential growth.

  Resulting Impact:

- The stock price rises from $50 to $75 within days due to the surge in demand.
- News channels, analysts, and social media amplify the excitement, encouraging even more buying activity.

Negative News: A Product Recall

A few months later, GreenDrive announces a recall of its EVs due to safety concerns with the new battery. The recall is expected to cost the company millions of dollars and delay future product launches.

Investor Reaction:

- Investors fear that the recall will harm GreenDrive's reputation and reduce future profits.
- Many shareholders decide to sell their stock to avoid potential losses.

  Resulting Impact:

- The stock price plummets from $75 to $40 in a single week as supply outpaces demand.
- Analysts lower their ratings for GreenDrive, further discouraging investors.

Mixed News: Earnings Report Surprises

During its quarterly earnings announcement, GreenDrive reports higher-than-expected revenue from existing models, but it also reveals that the recall has slowed new product development.

Investor Reaction:

- Some investors are optimistic because the revenue growth shows resilience.
- Others remain cautious due to delays in innovation.

Resulting Impact:

The stock price stabilizes at $60, reflecting a balance between optimism and caution.

Takeaway

- News plays a powerful role in influencing stock prices. Positive news can create buying pressure that drives prices up, while negative news often triggers selling pressure, causing prices to fall.
- Savvy investors pay attention to both company-specific news and broader market trends to make informed decisions.

Quick Quiz

Chapter 2: The Stock Market

1. Stock Exchanges: What is the key difference between the NASDAQ and NYSE?

    A. NASDAQ is physical, NYSE is electronic

    B. NASDAQ is tech-focused, NYSE has a trading floor

    C. NASDAQ is smaller than NYSE

    D. NASDAQ deals only in commodities

2. Market Function: If demand for a stock increase dramatically, what happens to its price?

    A. It decreases

    B. It remains the same

    C. It increases

    D. It depends on the stock exchange

3. Indexes: Which index tracks 500 of the largest U.S. companies?

    A. Dow Jones Industrial Average

    B. NASDAQ Composite

    C. S&P 500

    D. Russell 2000

CHAPTER 3

TYPES OF STOCKS AND INVESTMENT INSTRUMENTS

Investors have a variety of choices when it comes to building a stock portfolio. Understanding the types of stocks and investment instruments available is crucial for making informed decisions. This chapter explores the key types of stocks and introduces related investment tools like stock indexes, ETFs, mutual funds, and REITs.

Types of Stocks

1. Common Stocks

Definition: Common stocks represent ownership in a company. Holders typically have voting rights at shareholder meetings and may receive dividends.

Key Features:

- Voting rights.
- Variable dividends (paid only if the company profits).

Real-World Example:

Apple Inc. (AAPL): Investors who own Apple's common stock can vote on major company decisions, such as electing board members. Apple also pays quarterly dividends to its shareholders.

2. Preferred Stocks

Definition: Preferred stocks are a type of equity that typically do not grant voting rights but offer fixed dividends and priority over common stocks in case of bankruptcy.

Key Features:

- Higher dividend payments than common stocks.
- Priority over common stockholders in asset distribution.

Real-World Example:

Bank of America (BAC): Offers preferred stock with a fixed annual dividend yield, making it attractive for income-focused investors.

Characteristics of Stocks

1. Growth Stocks

Companies that reinvest profits to fuel future growth instead of paying dividends.

Real-World Example

Tesla Inc. (TSLA): Tesla focuses on innovation and expansion, reinvesting earnings into developing new products like self-driving technology rather than paying dividends.

2. Income Stocks

Companies that pay consistent dividends, providing investors with a steady income stream.

Real-World Example:

Procter & Gamble (PG): Known for paying reliable dividends for decades, appealing to investors seeking stable income.

3. Value Stocks

Stocks trading at a lower price relative to their fundamentals (e.g., earnings or dividends), often considered undervalued.

Real-World Example:

Ford Motor Company (F): Ford's low price-to-earnings (P/E) ratio compared to industry peers makes it a potential value stock for investors expecting a rebound.

4. Blue-Chip Stocks

Shares of large, financially sound, and established companies with a history of reliability and performance.

Real-World Example:

Microsoft (MSFT): As a leading technology company, Microsoft is widely regarded as a blue-chip stock due to its consistent performance and dividend payouts.

Extra: What is a Dividend Aristocrat?

Dividend Aristocrats, are a group of large-cap stocks in the S&P 500 that have increased their dividends for at least 25 years in a row

- They tend to be large, established companies that no longer enjoy supercharged growth.
- Many are largely recession-proof, enjoying steady profits and growing dividends in good times and bad.

Benefits

Dividend Aristocrats are "the best of the best" dividend growth stocks and have a history of outperforming the market. They are also considered to offer investors superior risk-adjusted returns

The list of Dividend Aristocrats is refreshed annually, with new companies added and those that no longer meet the criteria removed.

What is an ETF (Exchange-Traded Fund)?

ETFs are investment funds that trade on stock exchanges, containing a basket of stocks, bonds, or other assets.

Key Features:

- Offers diversification at a low cost.
- Traded like individual stocks.

Real-World Example:

SPDR S&P 500 ETF (SPY): Tracks the S&P 500 index, allowing investors to own shares of 500 companies in one trade.

What is a Mutual Fund?

A mutual fund pools money from many investors to invest in a diversified portfolio of stocks, bonds, or other securities, managed by professionals.

Key Features:

- Actively managed by fund managers.
- Offers diversification but may have higher fees than ETFs.

Real-World Example:

Vanguard 500 Index Fund (VFIAX): A mutual fund that mirrors the performance of the S&P 500.

What is a REIT (Real Estate Investment Trust)?

- REITs are companies that own, operate, or finance income-generating real estate, offering investors exposure to real estate markets without owning physical property.
- REITs invest in a wide scope of real estate property types, including offices, apartment buildings, warehouses, retail

centers, medical facilities, data centers, cell towers, infrastructure and hotels.

- Most REITs focus on a particular property type, but some hold multiple types of properties in their portfolios.

Types of REITs:

- **Equity REITs**: Own and manage properties (e.g., shopping malls, apartments).
- **Mortgage REITs**: Invest in real estate loans and mortgages.
- **Hybrid REITs**: Combine equity and mortgage REIT strategies.

Real-World Example:

Realty Income (O): A well-known equity REIT specializing in retail properties, paying monthly dividends.

Benefits of investing in REITs

Portfolio Diversification

REITs give real estate investors an opportunity to diversify their real estate holdings—something that's tough to do when you're buying individual investment properties, which requires a large amount of cash.

Accessibility

Investors who are interested in the real estate market don't have to save up tens of thousands of dollars for a sizable down payment on an investment property or make regular mortgage payments with REITs.

Passive Income

As a REIT shareholder, you'll receive regular dividends—monthly, quarterly or annually—based on your holding in the company.

Liquidity

- Unlike traditional real estate investments, REITs allow you to buy and sell shares by simply logging in to your brokerage account and making a trade.
- If you want to sell an investment property, on the other hand, it can take several months and a large amount of cash to make it happen. This liquidity gives you more flexibility in your investments, allowing you to access cash if you need to.

Competitive Returns

- In addition to regular income payments, REIT investors can also take advantage of price appreciation for their shares. Like stock prices, REIT prices can fluctuate over time.
- That said, a significant number of REITs outperform the stock market in terms of annualized returns, especially when you hold your position for 10 or more years.

Key Takeaway

There are a variety of investment options, from individual stocks & mutual funds to broader instruments like ETFs and REITs. Understanding these tools will enable you to build a portfolio tailored to your goals and risk tolerance. Choose the right combination of stocks and instruments based on your financial objectives and comfort with risk.

Quick Quiz

Chapter 3: Types of Stocks and Investment Instruments

1. Stock Types: Which type of stock typically provides voting rights and variable dividends?

   A. Preferred stocks

   B. Common stocks

   C. Growth stocks

   D. Income stocks

2. ETFs: What is one key advantage of investing in an ETF?

   A. Higher dividend yields than mutual funds

   B. Ability to trade like individual stocks

   C. Guaranteed returns

   D. No management fees

3. Real-World Example: If an investor buys shares of Realty Income (O), what type of investment are they making?

   A. A mutual fund

   B. A blue-chip stock

   C. A REIT

   D. A value stock

CHAPTER 4

KEY FINANCIAL METRICS

Key financial metrics help investors evaluate the performance and value of stocks. These metrics provide insights into a company's profitability, growth potential, and overall health.

This chapter explores essential metrics such as the Price-to-Earnings (P/E) ratio, dividend yield, and earnings per share (EPS), along with practical, real-world examples.

1. Price-to-Earnings (P/E) Ratio

Definition

The P/E ratio measures how much investors are willing to pay for each dollar of a company's earnings. It's a key metric for evaluating whether a stock is overvalued or undervalued.

Formula

P/E Ratio = Stock Price / Earnings Per Share

Real-World Example

Company: XYZ Inc.

Stock Price: $100

EPS: $5

Calculation:

P/E = 100 / 5 = 20

Interpretation:

- A P/E of 20 means investors are willing to pay $20 for every $1 of earnings.
- High P/E: Often indicates growth potential but may signal overvaluation.
- Low P/E: May suggest undervaluation or lack of growth expectations.

Comparison Example

- Company A (Tech Industry): P/E = 30 (high growth expectations).
- Company B (Utilities): P/E = 15 (steady but slow growth).

2. Dividend Yield

Definition

The dividend yield shows how much a company pays out in dividends relative to its stock price. It's an important metric for income-focused investors.

Formula

Dividend Yield = Annual Dividend / Stock Price × 100

Real-World Example

Company: ABC Corp.

Annual Dividend: $4

Stock Price: $80

Calculation:

Dividend Yield = 4 / 80 ×100

Interpretation:

- A dividend yield of 5% means investors earn $5 annually for every $100 invested.
- High Yield: May indicate a mature, income-focused company.
- Low Yield: Often seen in growth companies reinvesting profits.

Comparison Example

- Income Stock (Utility Company): 4-5% yield (e.g., Duke Energy).
- Growth Stock (Tech Company): 0-1% yield (e.g., Amazon).

3. Earnings Per Share (EPS)

Definition

EPS measures a company's profitability per share of stock. It's a direct indicator of a company's ability to generate profit for its shareholders.

Formula

EPS =Net Income / Number of Outstanding Shares

Real-World Example

Company: DEF Corp.

Net Income: $10 million

Outstanding Shares: 2 million

Calculation:

EPS = 10,000,000 / 2,000,000 = 5

Interpretation:

- An EPS of $5 means the company earned $5 for every share.
- Increasing EPS: Indicates growing profitability.
- Decreasing EPS: May signal declining performance.

Comparison Example

- Company A (High Growth): EPS = $8, steadily increasing each year.
- Company B (Declining): EPS = $3, showing year-over-year decline.

4. Return on Equity (ROE)

Definition

ROE measures how efficiently a company uses shareholder equity to generate profit.

Formula

ROE = Net Income / Shareholders' Equity × 100

Real-World Example

Company: GHI Ltd.

Net Income: $1.5 million

Shareholders' Equity: $10 million

Calculation:

ROE = 1,500,000 / 10,000,000 × 100 = 15%

Interpretation:

- A 15% ROE means the company generates $15 in profit for every $100 of shareholder equity.

- High ROE: Indicates efficient management.
- Low ROE: May signal inefficiencies.

5. Debt-to-Equity (D/E) Ratio

Definition

The D/E ratio assesses a company's financial leverage by comparing its total debt to shareholder equity.

Formula

D/E Ratio = Total Debt / Shareholders' Equity

Real-World Example

Company: JKL Inc.

Total Debt: $50 million

Shareholders' Equity: $100 million

Calculation:

D/E Ratio = 50,000,000 / 100,000,000 = 0.5

Interpretation:

- A D/E ratio of 0.5 means the company uses $0.50 of debt for every $1 of equity.
- Low D/E: Indicates conservative financial management.
- High D/E: Suggests higher risk.

Summary

- P/E Ratio: Helps evaluate whether a stock is overvalued or undervalued.
- Dividend Yield: Essential for income-focused investors.

- EPS: Measures profitability per share.
- ROE: Indicates how efficiently a company generates profit using shareholder equity.
- D/E Ratio: Shows the balance between debt and equity financing.

Quick Quiz

Chapter 4: Key Financial Metrics

1. P/E Ratio: If a company's stock price is $120 and its EPS is $10, what is its P/E ratio?

   A. 12

   B. 10

   C. 20

   D. 15

2. Dividend Yield: If a company pays an annual dividend of $2 and its stock price is $40, what is its dividend yield?

   A. 2%

   B. 4%

   C. 5%

   D. 6%

3. Financial Efficiency: What does a Return on Equity (ROE) of 20% signify?

   A. The company generates $20 in revenue for every $100 of shareholder equity.

   B. The company generates $20 in profit for every $100 of shareholder equity.

   C. The company owes $20 for every $100 of shareholder equity.

   D. The company has $20 in cash reserves.

CHAPTER 5

BEHAVIORAL ASPECTS OF INVESTING

Investing is not just about numbers, charts, and financial metrics. It's also deeply influenced by human psychology. Understanding the behavioral aspects of investing is crucial because emotions and cognitive biases often drive decisions that can hinder long-term success. This chapter explores common psychological pitfalls, the importance of discipline, and strategies to foster rational decision-making.

1. Emotional Biases in Investing

Fear and Greed

Two of the most powerful emotions in investing are fear and greed. These emotions often lead to impulsive decisions that can negatively impact investment outcomes.

- **Fear**: During market downturns, fear can drive investors to sell assets prematurely, locking in losses and missing out on potential recovery.
- **Greed**: When markets are booming, greed can push investors to chase trends or overextend themselves into risky investments.

Real-World Example: The 2008 Financial Crisis

During the 2008 financial crisis, the S&P 500 lost nearly 50% of its value. Many investors, driven by fear, sold their holdings at the market's lowest point. For example, John, a retail investor, sold his diversified portfolio in March 2009, fearing further losses. Within the next year, the market rebounded by over 60%, leaving John with significant unrealized losses. Conversely, those who remained disciplined and held onto their investments, such as Sarah, a long-term investor, saw their portfolios recover and even grow in subsequent years.

Real-World Example: The Dot-Com Bubble

In the late 1990s, greed fueled a surge in technology stock investments during the dot-com bubble. Investors piled into companies with little to no revenue, hoping for exponential growth. For example, Pets.com, a company with unsustainable business practices, saw its stock skyrocket before collapsing in 2000, leaving many investors with heavy losses. Those who conducted due diligence and avoided overvalued stocks fared better.

2. The Importance of Discipline and Long-Term Thinking

Focus on Goals

Successful investing requires clarity of purpose and a commitment to long-term objectives. Impulsive reactions to short-term market movements can derail even the best-laid plans.

The Power of Compounding

Long-term thinking allows investors to benefit from compounding—earning returns on both the initial investment and the accumulated gains.

Strategies for Discipline

- **Set a Plan**: Create an investment plan that aligns with your goals and risk tolerance.

- **Avoid Emotional Reactions**: Stick to your strategy, even during market volatility.
- **Periodic Reviews**: Evaluate your portfolio periodically to ensure it aligns with your objectives but avoid obsessively tracking daily market movements.

Real-World Example: Warren Buffett's Coca-Cola Investment

Warren Buffett purchased a significant stake in Coca-Cola in the late 1980s for approximately $1 billion. Despite market volatility, he held onto his investment, understanding the company's long-term value. By 2022, his investment had grown to over $25 billion, demonstrating the power of discipline and long-term thinking.

Real-World Example: Retirement Savings

Consider Jane, a 30-year-old who invests $5,000 annually in an S&P 500 index fund with an average annual return of 8%. By age 60, her portfolio grows to over $600,000, thanks to the compounding effect of consistent, disciplined investing. Conversely, Tom, who attempts to time the market and makes sporadic investments, ends up with a much smaller portfolio.

3. Avoiding "Herd Mentality" and Overtrading

Herd Mentality

Herd mentality occurs when individuals follow the actions of a larger group, often without independent analysis. This behavior can lead to market bubbles and crashes.

Example: The GameStop Stock Surge

In early 2021, GameStop's stock price surged from under $20 to over $400 due to a social media-driven buying frenzy.

Many retail investors bought in late, driven by herd mentality, only to see the stock plummet back to $40 within weeks. Those who entered without understanding the fundamentals suffered significant losses.

Overtrading

Frequent buying and selling of assets, often driven by short-term speculation or market noise, can erode returns through transaction costs and taxes.

Real-World Example: Day Trading Challenges

Michael, a novice investor, attempted day trading during a volatile market. Over six months, his frequent trades resulted in high transaction fees and taxable events. Despite initial gains, his portfolio underperformed compared to a simple buy-and-hold strategy due to the cumulative impact of costs.

Strategies to Avoid These Pitfalls

- **Independent Analysis**: Make decisions based on your research and not solely on trends.
- **Stay Educated**: Understand the fundamentals of your investments.
- **Limit Trading Activity**: Focus on holding quality investments for the long term.

Key Takeaway

The behavioral aspects of investing are as critical as the financial metrics. By recognizing emotional biases, maintaining discipline, and avoiding common psychological pitfalls like herd mentality and overtrading, investors can make more rational and informed decisions. Success in investing isn't just about what you know—it's also about how you behave. Master your mindset, and you'll be well-equipped to navigate the ups and downs of the market with confidence.

CHAPTER 6

HOW TO MAKE MONEY FROM STOCKS

The ultimate goal of investing in stocks is to make money. This can be achieved in two primary ways: capital gains and dividends. Each strategy has its advantages, depending on your financial goals and investment style. This chapter breaks down these methods and provides real-world examples to illustrate how they work.

1. Capital Gains

Definition: Capital gains occur when the price of a stock increases after you purchase it, and you sell it at a higher price than what you paid.

How It Works

- **Buying Low**: Purchase a stock at a relatively low price.
- **Selling High**: Wait for the stock's value to increase, then sell to realize the profit.

Real-World Example

- **Investor**: Alex purchases 100 shares of Tesla (TSLA) at $500 per share.
- **Total Investment**: $500 × 100 = $50,000.
- **Stock Price Increases**: Over 18 months, Tesla's stock price rises to $800 per share.

- **Total Value of Shares:** $800 × 100 = $80,000.
- **Outcome:**(Capital Gain): $80,000 - $50,000 = $30,000 (Net Profit).

Key Considerations

Holding Period:

- Short-term gains (held for less than a year) are taxed at higher rates.
- Long-term gains (held for more than a year) qualify for lower tax rates.

Market Timing: Successful capital gains depend on buying and selling at the right times.

2. Dividends

Definition: Dividends are payments made by companies to their shareholders, typically from their profits. These payments provide a steady income stream.

How It Works

- **Company Declares a Dividend**: A portion of the company's earnings are distributed to shareholders.
- **Investors Receive Payments**: Payments are typically made quarterly.

Real-World Example

- **Investor**: Sarah owns 500 shares of Procter & Gamble (PG), which pays an annual dividend of $3 per share.
- **Annual Dividend Income**: $3 × 500 = $1,500.
- **Reinvesting Dividends:**

- Sarah chooses to reinvest her dividends using a Dividend Reinvestment Plan (DRIP).
- At a stock price of $150, her $1,500 dividend buys an additional 10 shares of PG.

Key Considerations

- **Dividend Yield**: Higher yields often mean higher income but may signal less growth potential.
- **Reliable Income**: Dividends can provide stability during market downturns.

3. Combining Capital Gains and Dividends

Many investors combine these strategies to balance growth and income.

Real-World Example

- **Investor**: David invests $20,000 in a balanced portfolio:
  - 60% in growth stocks like Amazon (AMZN) for capital gains.
  - 40% in dividend-paying stocks like Coca-Cola (KO) for regular income.
- **Results After One Year**:
  - Growth Stocks: Gain of $3,000 from price increases.
  - Dividend Stocks: $1,200 in dividend income.
- Total Earnings: $3,000 (capital gains) + $1,200 (dividends) = $4,200.

4. Risks and Challenges

While the potential to make money is significant, there are risks:

- **Market Volatility**: Stock prices can fluctuate, causing losses if you sell during a downturn.

- **Dividend Cuts**: Companies may reduce or eliminate dividends during financial hardships.
- **Emotional Decision-Making**: Fear and greed can lead to poor timing on buying or selling.

5. Advanced Strategies (Optional)

For investors who have mastered the basics, advanced strategies offer additional ways to generate returns. These methods often involve higher risks and require a deeper understanding of the market. While this book introduces these concepts briefly, they will be explored in detail in a future series.

A. Options Trading

Definition: Options are contracts that give investors the right, but not the obligation, to buy or sell a stock at a specific price within a set time frame.

Key Types of Options:

- **Call Options**: The right to buy a stock at a specified price (useful when you expect the price to rise).
- **Put Options**: The right to sell a stock at a specified price (useful when you expect the price to fall).

Example – Covered Call Strategy:

- You own 100 shares of Microsoft (MSFT), trading at $300 per share.
- You sell a call option with a strike price of $320, earning a premium of $5 per share ($500 total).
- If the stock stays below $320, you keep your shares and the premium. If it rises above $320, you sell your shares at a profit.

B. Short Selling

Definition: Short selling involves borrowing shares of a stock and selling them with the expectation that the price will fall. Later, you buy the shares back at a lower price to return to the lender, keeping the difference as profit.

Example:

- You believe Stock XYZ, currently trading at $50, will drop in value.
- You borrow 100 shares and sell them for $5,000.
- When the stock price falls to $40, you buy back the 100 shares for $4,000, returning them to the lender and earning a $1,000 profit.

Risks:

Unlimited Loss Potential: If the stock price rises instead of falling, losses can be substantial.

C. Margin Trading

Definition: Margin trading involves borrowing money from your broker to purchase more stocks than you could with your own funds, amplifying potential gains and losses.

Example:

- You invest $5,000 of your own money and borrow an additional $5,000 on margin to buy $10,000 worth of stock.
- If the stock rises 10%, your return on investment doubles to 20% due to leverage.
- However, if the stock falls 10%, your losses also double.

D. Hedging

Definition: Hedging involves using financial instruments, like options or futures, to reduce potential losses in your portfolio.

Example:

- You own shares of a tech company and fear a market downturn.
- To protect your portfolio, you buy put options, allowing you to sell your shares at a predetermined price if the stock falls.

E. Day Trading

Definition: Day trading involves buying and selling stocks within the same trading day to profit from small price movements.

Example:

A day trader buys 1,000 shares of Company ABC at $50 in the morning and sells them at $51 in the afternoon, earning a quick $1,000 profit (minus fees).

NOTE: Advanced strategies like options trading, short selling, and margin trading can offer higher returns but come with significantly higher risks. These techniques are best suited for experienced investors with a thorough understanding of the market.

Takeaway

Investors can make money from stocks through capital gains by selling shares at a higher price or through dividends that provide regular income. A balanced approach combining both strategies can create a robust portfolio. However, success requires understanding the market, patience, and a clear investment plan.

Quick Quiz

Chapter 6: How to Make Money from Stocks

1. Capital Gains: If you buy 100 shares of a stock at $50 each and sell them at $70 each, what is your total capital gain?

   A. $1,000

   B. $2,000

   C. $5,000

   D. $7,000

2. Dividends: If a company pays a dividend of $3 per share and you own 200 shares, how much annual income will you receive?

   A. $200

   B. $300

   C. $600

   D. $1,200

3. Combined Strategies: What is a potential benefit of combining capital gains and dividend income?

   A. Guaranteed returns

   B. Diversified income streams

   C. Lower tax rates

   D. Risk-free investing

CHAPTER 7

RISKS AND CONSIDERATIONS

Investing in stocks offers the potential for high returns, but it also comes with risks. Understanding these risks is crucial to making informed decisions and managing your portfolio effectively. This chapter explores key risks and provides strategies to mitigate them.

1. Market Risk

Definition: Market risk refers to the potential for stock prices to decline due to factors affecting the entire market, such as economic downturns, geopolitical events, or changes in interest rates.

Real-World Example: 2008 Financial Crisis

- During the global financial crisis, the S&P 500 lost nearly 50% of its value between October 2007 and March 2009.
- Even fundamentally strong companies saw their stock prices plummet due to widespread panic and economic uncertainty.

Mitigation Strategies

- Diversify across sectors and asset classes.
- Avoid panic selling during downturns by focusing on long-term goals.

2. Company-Specific Risk

Definition: This risk arises from issues specific to an individual company, such as poor management, declining sales, or product recalls.

Real-World Example: Boeing's 737 MAX Crisis

- In 2019, Boeing faced significant losses after two crashes involving its 737 MAX aircraft.
- The stock price fell by over 25% within months as airlines canceled orders and regulators grounded the planes.

Mitigation Strategies

- Research a company's financial health, leadership, and industry position before investing.
- Limit exposure to a single stock to avoid concentration risk.

3. Volatility Risk

Definition: Volatility refers to the rapid and unpredictable changes in stock prices, which can lead to significant short-term losses or gains.

Real-World Example: Tesla (TSLA)

Tesla's stock has experienced extreme price swings. In 2020, it gained over 700% due to investor optimism but also saw sharp drops of 20% or more during corrections.

Mitigation Strategies

- Invest in stable, less volatile stocks for conservative portfolios.
- Use dollar-cost averaging to spread purchases over time, reducing the impact of market fluctuations.

What is dollar-cost averaging?

Dollar-cost averaging (DCA) is an investment strategy where you invest a fixed amount of money at regular intervals, regardless of the current market price, essentially buying more shares when the price is low and fewer when it's high, which helps lower your average cost per share over time and mitigate the impact of market volatility; it's a way to consistently put money into the market without trying to time the market perfectly.

4. Liquidity Risk

Definition: Liquidity risk occurs when it's difficult to buy or sell a stock without significantly impacting its price, often seen with smaller companies or low-trading-volume stocks.

Real-World Example: Small-Cap Stock Challenges

- A small biotech company might see limited trading activity.
- If you own a significant number of shares and decide to sell, the lack of buyers could drive the price down, reducing your returns.

Mitigation Strategies

- Focus on investing in liquid stocks with high trading volumes.
- Avoid overinvesting in small-cap or niche-market stocks.

5. Inflation Risk

What is inflation?

Inflation is a general increase in the price of goods and services over time. It can also be described as a decrease in the value of a currency.

Real-World Example: 1970s Stagflation

During periods of high inflation in the 1970s, the real returns on many investments were negative, as inflation outpaced stock price growth.

Mitigation Strategies

- Invest in stocks that historically outperform during inflationary periods, such as utility or energy stocks and consumer staples.

What are consumer staples?

Consumer staples are essential products that people buy regularly, regardless of their financial situation or the state of the economy. Examples of consumer staples include Food and beverages, Household goods, Hygiene products, Alcohol, and Tobacco.

6. Emotional Risk

Definition: Emotional risk arises when investors make decisions based on fear, greed, or market noise instead of rational analysis.

Real-World Example: Selling During the COVID-19 Crash

- In March 2020, markets experienced a sharp decline due to COVID-19 fears.
- Many investors sold their holdings in panic, missing the subsequent recovery where the S&P 500 gained over 70% by the end of the year.

Mitigation Strategies

- Develop a clear investment plan and stick to it, regardless of short-term market fluctuations.
- Avoid checking portfolio performance too frequently to reduce stress-driven decisions.

7. Regulatory and Political Risk

Definition: Changes in government policies, regulations, or geopolitical tensions can impact stock performance.

Real-World Example: Tariffs During the U.S.-China Trade War

In 2018, tariffs imposed during the U.S.-China trade war caused volatility in technology and manufacturing stocks, with companies like Apple and Caterpillar experiencing significant price swings.

Mitigation Strategies

- Monitor political and regulatory developments that could impact your investments.
- Diversify globally to reduce reliance on any single country's market.

Takeaway

Investing in stocks involves risks that can significantly impact your portfolio's value. By understanding these risks and implementing strategies like diversification, research, and emotional discipline, investors can minimize losses and position themselves for long-term success.

Quick Quiz

Chapter 7: Risks and Considerations

1. Market Risk: What is an example of market risk?

   A. A company faces declining sales.

   B. Stock prices drop due to an economic recession.

   C. A company's CEO resigns unexpectedly.

   D. A company announces a product recall.

2. Volatility Risk: If a stock experiences frequent sharp price increases and decreases, it is considered:

   A. Stable

   B. Overvalued

   C. Volatile

   D. Undervalued

3. Diversification: How does diversification help reduce risk?

   A. It guarantees higher returns.

   B. It spreads investments across different asset types.

   C. It eliminates losses completely.

   D. It focuses investments on one industry.

CHAPTER 8

SECTORS AND INDUSTRIES

The stock market is often divided into sectors and industries, which represent different parts of the economy. Understanding these categories can help investors diversify their portfolios, identify opportunities, and make informed decisions based on market conditions. This chapter explores the major sectors, the importance of sector diversification, and the difference between cyclical and defensive industries.

1. Overview of Sectors

Sectors are broad categories that group companies based on the type of business they operate. Within each sector, there are more specific industries.

Major Stock Market Sectors

A. **Technology**: Companies that develop software, hardware, and IT services. Example: Apple, Microsoft.

B. **Healthcare**: Providers of medical services, pharmaceuticals, and biotechnology. Example: Pfizer, UnitedHealth Group.

C. **Energy**: Companies involved in oil, gas, and renewable energy. Example: ExxonMobil, NextEra Energy.

D. **Financials**: Banks, insurance companies, and investment firms. Example: JPMorgan Chase, Berkshire Hathaway.

E. **Consumer Discretionary**: Non-essential goods and services like retail, automotive, and entertainment. Example: Tesla, Nike.

F. **Consumer Staples**: Essential goods such as food, beverages, and household products. Example: Procter & Gamble, Coca-Cola.

G. **Utilities**: Providers of essential services like electricity, water, and natural gas. Example: Duke Energy, Dominion Energy.

H. **Industrials**: Companies that manufacture goods or provide industrial services. Example: Boeing, Caterpillar.

I. **Materials**: Producers of raw materials like metals, chemicals, and forestry products. Example: Dow Inc., Newmont Corporation.

J. **Real Estate**: Real estate investment trusts (REITs) and property management. Example: Realty Income, Simon Property Group.

K. **Communication Services**: Providers of telecom and media services. Example: Verizon, Netflix.

2. How to Diversify by Sector

Diversification by sector reduces risk by spreading investments across different parts of the economy. This ensures that poor performance in one sector doesn't disproportionately impact the portfolio.

Steps to Diversify

1. **Assess Sector Exposure**: Use tools like sector ETFs to understand your current exposure.

2. **Balance Growth and Stability**: Include sectors with high growth potential (e.g., technology) and stable performance (e.g., consumer staples).
3. **Adjust for Market Conditions**: Shift allocation based on economic trends or personal goals.

Real-World Example: A Balanced Portfolio

John creates a $100,000 portfolio with exposure to multiple sectors:

- **Technology (20%)**: Invests $20,000 in the Invesco QQQ ETF for high growth potential.
- **Healthcare (15%):** Allocates $15,000 to Pfizer and Johnson & Johnson for stability and innovation.
- **Consumer Staples (10%):** Buys $10,000 in Coca-Cola for steady returns.
- **Energy (10%):** Puts $10,000 in ExxonMobil for dividend income.
- **Real Estate (10%):** Invests $10,000 in Realty Income for exposure to property markets.
- **Financials (15%):** Allocates $15,000 to JPMorgan Chase for stability and dividends.
- **Remaining 20%:** Distributed among utilities, industrials, and communication services to round out the portfolio.

3. Cyclical vs. Defensive Industries

Cyclical Industries

- These industries are highly sensitive to economic changes. They perform well during economic growth and poorly during recessions.

- **Examples:** Automotive, travel, luxury goods.
- **Companies:** Tesla (automotive), Carnival Cruise Line (travel).

Defensive Industries

- These industries remain stable regardless of economic conditions. They provide essential goods and services.
- **Examples:** Utilities, healthcare, consumer staples.
- **Companies:** Procter & Gamble (consumer staples), Duke Energy (utilities).

Real-World Example: Economic Impact on Industries

During the COVID-19 pandemic in 2020, cyclical industries like travel and hospitality faced significant downturns as global restrictions halted activity. Companies like Delta Airlines and Carnival Cruise Line saw sharp declines in revenue and stock prices. Meanwhile, defensive industries like healthcare and consumer staples thrived. Companies such as Clorox and Pfizer experienced increased demand for cleaning products and vaccines, leading to stock price appreciation.

Takeaway

Understanding sectors and industries is a critical part of investment strategy. Diversifying across sectors helps mitigate risk, while recognizing the differences between cyclical and defensive industries allows investors to adapt to varying market conditions. By analyzing sector performance and aligning it with personal goals, investors can build a robust and resilient portfolio.

CHAPTER 9

GETTING STARTED

Investing in the stock market may seem intimidating at first, but with the right approach, anyone can get started. This chapter provides a step-by-step guide to begin your investing journey, including setting financial goals, understanding risk tolerance, choosing a brokerage, conducting research, and monitoring your investments.

1. Setting Financial Goals

Before investing, determine what you want to achieve and the timeframe for reaching your goals. Clear goals help you choose the right investments.

Types of Goals

- **Short-Term Goals** (1-5 years): Saving for a vacation, car, or emergency fund.
- **Medium-Term Goals** (5-10 years): Saving for a down payment on a house or starting a business.
- **Long-Term Goals** (10+ years): Building retirement savings or creating generational wealth.

Real-World Example

Investor: Emma, a 30-year-old professional, wants to save $50,000 for a down payment on a home in five years. To achieve this:

- She invests $800 monthly in a mix of conservative ETFs and dividend-paying stocks.
- She selects investments that historically provide steady growth of 5-7% annually.
- After five years, her portfolio grows to approximately $52,200, helping her reach her goal.

2. Understanding Risk Tolerance

Definition: Risk tolerance refers to your ability and willingness to handle fluctuations in your investments' value.

Categories of Risk Tolerance

- **Conservative:** Prefers stable, low-risk investments like bonds or dividend stocks.
- **Moderate:** Comfortable with a mix of stocks and bonds for balanced growth.
- **Aggressive:** Seeks high returns by investing in growth stocks or emerging markets.

Real-World Example

Investor: Daniel, a 25-year-old with a stable income and no major financial obligations, has a high-risk tolerance. He invests 80% of his portfolio in growth stocks like Tesla (TSLA) and Amazon (AMZN), and 20% in ETFs for diversification. This allocation suits his long-term wealth-building goals.

Risk Tolerance Assessment Tool

To assess your risk tolerance, answer these questions:

- What is your investment timeframe? (Short-term, medium-term, long-term)
- How would you react to a 10-20% market downturn?

- Are you comfortable taking higher risks for potentially higher returns?
- Do you rely on your investments for immediate income?

Tools like 'Vanguards Risk Tolerance Questionnaire or 'Fidelitys Investment Profile Quiz can provide additional guidance.

3. Choosing a Brokerage Account

Definition: A brokerage account is a platform that allows you to buy and sell stocks, ETFs, mutual funds, and other securities.

Types of Brokers

- **Full-Service Brokers**
  - Offer personalized advice and financial planning.
  - Higher fees; suitable for investors who want guidance.
  - Examples: Merrill Lynch, Edward Jones.
- **Online Brokers**
  - Low-cost, self-directed platforms for independent investors.
  - Examples: Robinhood, Fidelity, Charles Schwab.

Real-World Example

Investor: Sophia, a beginner, chooses Fidelity for its extensive educational resources and low-cost trading. She opens an individual brokerage account, deposits $1,000, and begins investing in ETFs to diversify her portfolio.

4. Conducting Stock Research

Definition: Researching stocks involves analyzing a company's performance, industry trends, and market conditions before investing.

Sources for Stock Research

- **Company Reports**: Read quarterly and annual reports (e.g., 10-K filings) to assess financial health.
- **Stock Screeners**: Tools like Yahoo Finance, Morningstar, and Zacks help filter stocks based on metrics like P/E ratio and market cap.
- **News Outlets**: Follow reputable sources such as Bloomberg, CNBC, or the Wall Street Journal.
- **Analyst Ratings**: Review ratings and price targets from professional analysts.

Real-World Example

Investor: Mark is interested in investing in Starbucks (SBUX). He:

- Reads the annual report to learn about its global expansion strategy.
- Uses Yahoo Finance to analyze financial metrics, including a P/E ratio of 28.
- Checks recent news and finds strong quarterly earnings results.
- Decides to invest, expecting steady growth from Starbucks' global presence.

5. Placing Your First Trade

Order Types

- **Market Order**
  - Executes immediately at the current market price.
  - **Pros**: Guaranteed execution.

- **Cons**: May not get the desired price during volatile markets.
- **Example**: You place a market order to buy 10 shares of Apple (AAPL) at $150. The order is filled instantly, but the final price could vary slightly due to real-time market changes.

- **Limit Order**
  - Executes only at a specified price or better.
  - **Pros**: Greater control over the price.
  - **Cons**: The order may not be executed if the stock doesn't reach the desired price.
  - **Example**: You place a limit order to buy 10 shares of Apple (AAPL) at $145. If the stock price drops to $145, the order is executed; otherwise, it remains pending.

6. Starting Small with Dollar-Cost Averaging

Definition: Dollar-cost averaging (DCA) involves investing a fixed amount of money regularly, regardless of market prices.

Real-World Example

Investor: Alex invests $200 per month in the SPDR S&P 500 ETF (SPY):

- **Month 1**: SPY is $400; Alex buys 0.5 shares.
- **Month 2**: SPY drops to $350; Alex buys 0.57 shares.
- **Month 3**: SPY rises to $450; Alex buys 0.44 shares.

Over time, Alex accumulates more shares at an average cost, reducing the impact of short-term volatility.

7. Monitoring Your Investments

Why Monitor Investments?

Regular monitoring ensures your portfolio aligns with your goals and adapts to market changes.

Monitoring Timeframe

- **Monthly**: Ideal for active investors tracking short-term goals.
- **Quarterly**: Suitable for long-term investors who make fewer adjustments.

What to Look For

- **Performance Metrics**: Compare each stock's performance to benchmarks like the S&P 500.
- **Portfolio Balance**: Ensure diversification across sectors and asset classes.
- **Market Changes**: Review how economic trends or company-specific news impact your holdings.

Best Practices

- Set calendar reminders for regular reviews.
- Avoid emotional reactions to short-term volatility.
- Rebalance your portfolio annually or as needed.

What does rebalancing your portfolio mean?

Rebalancing a portfolio is the process of buying or selling assets to realign the weightings of a portfolio to meet financial goals and risk tolerance. The goal is to maintain the desired asset allocation and risk level, and to help manage risk and volatility.

Here's an example of rebalancing a portfolio:

- **Original allocation**: An investor's target allocation is 80% stocks and 20% bonds.
- **After some time**: The stock portfolio performs well and the stock weighting increases to 90%.
- **Rebalancing**: The investor sells some stocks and buys bonds to get the portfolio back to the original 80/20 allocation.

Rebalancing a portfolio can help with:

- Maintaining the desired risk-return profile
- Booking profits on high-value assets
- Buying undervalued assets
- Revising the portfolio allocation if financial goals or risk tolerance change

Rebalancing is especially important during times of significant market volatility.

Real-World Example

Investor: Maria notices her tech-heavy portfolio outperformed during a market rally but is now overexposed to risk. She:

- Sells part of her tech holdings.
- Reallocates to defensive sectors like healthcare and utilities.
- Maintains a balanced portfolio aligned with her risk tolerance.

Takeaway

Getting started in the stock market requires setting clear financial goals, understanding your risk tolerance, and choosing the right brokerage. Conduct thorough research, use tools like dollar-cost averaging, and monitor your portfolio regularly to ensure it stays aligned with your financial objectives. By following these steps, you'll build a solid foundation for long-term investment success.

Quick Quiz

Chapter 9: Getting Started

1. Risk Tolerance: What type of investor would prefer bonds and dividend-paying stocks?

   A. Conservative

   B. Aggressive

   C. Speculative

   D. Moderate

2. Brokerage Accounts: Which type of broker is best for beginners seeking low fees and educational resources?

   A. Full-service broker

   B. Online broker

   C. Robo-advisor

   D. Investment bank

3. Dollar-Cost Averaging: What is one advantage of dollar-cost averaging?

   A. It guarantees profits.

   B. It eliminates the need for diversification.

   C. It reduces the impact of market volatility.

   D. It requires less initial capital.

CHAPTER 10

STOCK INVESTMENT STRATEGIES

Stock investment strategies are frameworks investors use to make decisions about buying, holding, and selling stocks. These strategies vary based on individual goals, risk tolerance, and time horizons. In this chapter, we'll explore key strategies with detailed examples and tips for implementation.

1. Buy and Hold Strategy

Definition: The buy and hold strategy involves purchasing stocks and holding them for an extended period, regardless of short-term market fluctuations. This approach is ideal for long-term investors.

Key Features

- Focuses on long-term growth.
- Relies on the power of compounding.
- Avoids frequent trading and transaction fees.

Real-World Example

Investor: Sarah purchased 50 shares of Apple (AAPL) in 2010 at $30 per share. Over the next decade, Apple introduced innovative products like the iPhone and iPad, driving its stock price to $150 in 2020.

- **Initial Investment:** $1,500 (50 shares × $30/share).
- **Value After 10 Years:** $7,500 (50 shares × $150/share).
- **Total Gain:** $6,000.
- **Takeaway:** Sarah's patience allowed her to benefit from Apple's long-term growth without reacting to short-term market volatility.

2. Dollar-Cost Averaging (DCA)

Definition: Dollar-cost averaging involves investing a fixed amount of money at regular intervals, regardless of market prices. This strategy reduces the impact of market volatility.

Key Features

- Mitigates the risk of investing a lump sum at the wrong time.
- Encourages disciplined investing.
- Reduces emotional decision-making.

Real-World Example

Investor: Alex invests $200 monthly in the Vanguard Total Stock Market ETF (VTI):

- **Month 1:** VTI is $200; Alex buys 1 share.
- **Month 2:** VTI drops to $180; Alex buys 1.11 shares.
- **Month 3:** VTI rises to $220; Alex buys 0.91 shares.
- **Average Price Paid:** $200 ÷ 3 = $200.
- **Shares Accumulated:** 3.02 shares.
- **Takeaway:** By consistently investing, Alex accumulates shares at varying prices, reducing the impact of short-term market fluctuations.

3. Growth Investing

Definition: Growth investing focuses on companies expected to grow faster than the overall market. These companies often reinvest profits into expansion rather than paying dividends.

Key Features

- High potential for capital appreciation.
- Often involves higher risk due to valuation premiums.
- Suitable for investors with a higher risk tolerance.

Real-World Example

Investor: Emily invested $10,000 in Tesla (TSLA) in 2018 when the stock price was $70. By 2021, Tesla's stock price soared to $700 due to increased demand for electric vehicles.

- **Initial Investment:** $10,000 / $70 = 143 shares.
- **Value in 2021:** 143 shares × $700 = $100,100.
- **Total Gain:** $90,100.
- **Takeaway:** Growth investing in innovative companies like Tesla can yield significant returns but requires tolerance for volatility.

4. Value Investing

Definition: Value investing focuses on buying undervalued stocks with strong fundamentals, often trading below their intrinsic value.

Key Features

- Relies on financial analysis to identify undervalued stocks.
- Seeks a margin of safety to minimize risk.
- Popularized by Warren Buffett.

Real-World Example

Investor: John purchased shares of Coca-Cola (KO) in 2009 during the global financial crisis when the stock was undervalued at $20 per share. By 2020, the stock price had risen to $60.

- **Initial Investment:** $5,000 / $20 = 250 shares.
- **Value in 2020:** 250 shares × $60 = $15,000.
- **Total Gain:** $10,000.
- **Takeaway:** John's ability to identify undervalued stocks and hold them for the long term resulted in substantial returns.

5. Dividend Investing

Definition: Dividend investing focuses on companies that regularly distribute a portion of their profits to shareholders. This strategy emphasizes income generation.

Key Features

- Provides consistent income.
- Suitable for conservative or income-focused investors.
- Often involves mature, stable companies.

Real-World Example

Investor: David owns 1,000 shares of AT&T (T), which pays an annual dividend of $2 per share.

- **Annual Dividend Income:** 1,000 shares × $2/share = $2,000.
- **Reinvested Dividends:** David uses a Dividend Reinvestment Plan (DRIP) to buy additional shares, compounding his returns over time.

- **Takeaway:** Dividend investing provides a reliable income stream and can enhance returns when dividends are reinvested.

6. Building a Balanced Portfolio

Definition: A balanced portfolio includes a mix of asset classes, such as stocks, bonds, and cash, tailored to an investor's risk tolerance and goals.

Key Features

- Reduces overall portfolio risk.
- Provides diversification across sectors and asset types.
- Aligns with long-term financial goals.

Real-World Example

Investor: Rachel allocates her $100,000 portfolio as follows:

- 60% in stocks (growth and value stocks).
- 30% in bonds for stability.
- 10% in cash for liquidity.
- **Performance:** During a market downturn, Rachel's bonds cushion losses from declining stock prices, preserving her portfolio's value.
- **Takeaway:** A balanced portfolio helps investors navigate market volatility and achieve steady growth.

Takeaway

Stock investment strategies are tools to align your portfolio with your financial goals, risk tolerance, and time horizon. Whether you focus on long-term growth, income, or value, the key to success lies in consistency, discipline, and regular portfolio reviews. Choose a strategy that complements your goals and stay committed for long-term success.

CHAPTER 11

INTERACTIVE EXERCISES

Interactive exercises are a powerful way to apply what you've learned about stock investing. This chapter includes practical activities to help you create a sample portfolio, track stock performance, and analyze real-world case studies. These exercises are designed to enhance your confidence and understanding of the stock market.

1. Creating a Sample Portfolio

Objective: Learn how to build a diversified portfolio tailored to your goals and risk tolerance.

Instructions

1. **Define Your Goals**: Decide whether you want growth, income, or a mix of both.
2. **Allocate Assets**: Use the following sample allocation based on risk tolerance:
    - **Conservative**: 30% stocks, 50% bonds, 20% cash.
    - **Moderate**: 60% stocks, 30% bonds, 10% cash.
    - **Aggressive**: 80% stocks, 15% bonds, 5% cash.
3. **Research and Select Stocks**:
    - Pick at least five companies from different industries (e.g., tech, healthcare, consumer goods).

- Use financial metrics like P/E ratio, dividend yield, and growth rate to guide your choices.

4. **Allocate Funds**: Decide how much money to invest in each stock.

Real-World Example: Moderate Portfolio

Investor: Alex creates a $10,000 portfolio with the following allocation:

- Apple (AAPL): $2,000 (tech sector).
- Procter & Gamble (PG): $2,000 (consumer goods).
- Johnson & Johnson (JNJ): $2,000 (healthcare).
- Vanguard S&P 500 ETF (VOO): $3,000 (diversified fund).
- U.S. Treasury Bonds: $1,000 (fixed income).

Outcome: Alex's diversified portfolio balances growth and stability, aligning with his moderate risk tolerance.

Real-World Example: Conservative Portfolio

Investor: Maria, a retiree, creates a $50,000 conservative portfolio focusing on stability and income:

- Vanguard Total Bond Market ETF (BND): $25,000 (50% bonds).
- Coca-Cola (KO): $10,000 (20% stocks, consumer goods with a strong dividend history).
- Johnson & Johnson (JNJ): $5,000 (10% stocks, healthcare with consistent growth).
- Cash Reserve: $10,000 (20% for liquidity and emergency needs).

Outcome: Maria's portfolio minimizes risk while generating steady income through dividends and bond interest.

Real-World Example: Aggressive Portfolio

Investor: Ethan, a 25-year-old with a high-risk tolerance, builds a $15,000 aggressive portfolio aiming for long-term growth:

- Tesla (TSLA): $5,000 (33% in growth-oriented tech).
- NVIDIA (NVDA): $4,000 (27% in cutting-edge AI and graphics technologies).
- ARK Innovation ETF (ARKK): $3,000 (20% in a diversified, high-risk ETF).
- Coinbase (COIN): $2,000 (13% in cryptocurrency exposure).
- Cash Reserve: $1,000 (7% for opportunistic investments).

Outcome: Ethan's portfolio focuses on high-growth sectors, accepting greater volatility for the potential of higher returns.

2. Tracking Stock Performance

Objective: Learn how to monitor the performance of your investments and interpret key metrics.

Instructions

1. Select three stocks from your sample portfolio.
2. Record the following data weekly for three months:
   - Stock price.
   - Percentage change in price.

- Dividends received (if applicable).
- Relevant news impacting the stock.

3. Analyze performance trends and identify patterns.

Real-World Example

Investor: Emma tracks her holdings in Tesla (TSLA), Coca-Cola (KO), and Amazon (AMZN):

- Tesla's stock price rose 15% due to strong quarterly earnings.
- Coca-Cola provides a consistent dividend yield of 3%.
- Amazon's price fluctuates but recovers after a positive product launch.

Outcome: Emma learns how external factors like earnings reports and market sentiment affect her portfolio.

3. Analyzing Case Studies of Successful Companies

Objective: Understand the factors that contribute to a company's long-term success.

Instructions

1. Choose a well-known company that has performed well over the past decade (e.g., Apple, Microsoft, or Starbucks).
2. Research the following:
   - Key milestones (e.g., product launches, acquisitions).
   - Revenue and earnings growth trends.
   - Stock price growth and volatility.
3. Identify the strategies that contributed to the company's success.

Real-World Example

Company: Apple Inc. (AAPL)

- **Key Milestones:** Launch of the iPhone in 2007 and transition to subscription services (Apple Music, iCloud).
- **Revenue Growth:** Increased from $65 billion in 2010 to over $365 billion in 2021.
- **Stock Price Growth:** Rose from $10 (split-adjusted) in 2010 to over $150 in 2021.

Outcome: Apple's focus on innovation, branding, and recurring revenue streams illustrates why it remains a market leader.

4. Simulating a Market Scenario

Objective: Experience decision-making in a simulated market environment.

Instructions

1. Create a hypothetical scenario (e.g., a market downturn or a booming economy).
2. Make decisions for your sample portfolio:
   - Should you buy, hold, or sell each stock?
   - How do market conditions affect your decisions?
3. Reflect on the outcome of your decisions.

Real-World Example

Scenario: A recession leads to a 20% drop in stock prices.

Alex decides to:

- Hold Apple and Johnson & Johnson for long-term growth.
- Buy more shares of the Vanguard S&P 500 ETF at a lower price.
- Avoid selling any stocks to prevent locking in losses.

Outcome: By staying disciplined, Alex positions his portfolio for recovery when the market rebounds.

Takeaway

Interactive exercises provide practical experience and deepen your understanding of stock investing. By creating a sample portfolio, tracking performance, analyzing case studies, and simulating market scenarios, you'll build confidence and develop the skills needed to make informed investment decisions. Consistent practice is key to becoming a successful investor.

CHAPTER 12

ADDITIONAL RESOURCES AND GLOSSARY OF KEY TERMS

This chapter provides valuable additional resources for continuous learning about investing and a glossary of essential terms to reinforce your understanding. The glossary includes clear, concise definitions to help you navigate the stock market with confidence.

Additional Resources

Books

- A Random Walk Down Wall Street by Burton Malkiel: Covers various investment strategies and the importance of diversification.
- Common Stocks and Uncommon Profits by Philip Fisher: Insights on growth investing and understanding a company's business.
- The Intelligent Investor by Benjamin Graham: A classic guide to value investing and long-term strategies.

Websites and Tools

- BlackEnterprise.com: The centerpiece of BLACK ENTERPRISE content is our Wealth For Life initiative.
- Investopedia: A comprehensive educational resource for investing terms and strategies.

- Morningstar: Offers in-depth analysis and ratings for stocks, ETFs, and mutual funds.
- Nareit: Nareit is the leading producer and sponsor of research on REIT investment
- SEC's EDGAR Database: Access company filings for detailed financial reports.
- WealthBuilders Community: a private community that shows you how to confidently build wealth, so that you can live a stress free, debt free, and financially free life.
- Yahoo Finance: Provides real-time stock prices, news, and financial data.

Apps

- Acorns: Simplifies investing through automated portfolio contributions.
- Fidelity: Comprehensive investment tools and research resources.
- Robinhood: User-friendly platform for trading stocks and ETFs.

Glossary of Key Terms

Blue-Chip Stocks

Blue-chip stocks are shares of large, well-established, and financially sound companies with a history of reliability and stable growth. Example: Microsoft (MSFT).

Brokerage Account

A brokerage account is a platform that allows you to buy and sell stocks, ETFs, mutual funds, and other securities.

Capital Gains

Capital gains refer to the profit earned when you sell an asset, such as a stock, for a higher price than what you paid. Example: Buying a stock at $50 and selling it at $70 yields a capital gain of $20.

Common Stocks

Definition: Common stocks represent ownership in a company. Holders typically have voting rights at shareholder meetings and may receive dividends.

Consumer Staples

Consumer staples are essential products that people buy regularly, regardless of their financial situation or the state of the economy. Examples include food and beverages, household goods, hygiene products, alcohol, and tobacco.

Debt-to-Equity (D/E) Ratio

The D/E ratio assesses a company's financial leverage by comparing its total debt to shareholder equity.

Formula: D/E Ratio = Total Debt / Shareholders' Equity

Dividend

Dividends are payments made by companies to their shareholders, typically from their profits. These payments provide a steady income stream.

Dividend Aristocrat

Dividend Aristocrats are a group of large-cap stocks in the S&P 500 that have increased their dividends for at least 25 years in a row. Example: Procter & Gamble (PG).

Dividend Yield

The dividend yield shows how much a company pays out in dividends relative to its stock price. It's an important metric for income-focused investors.

Formula: Dividend Yield = Annual Dividend / Stock Price × 100

Dollar-Cost Averaging (DCA)

Dollar-cost averaging (DCA) is an investment strategy where you invest a fixed amount of money at regular intervals, regardless of the current market price. This helps lower your average cost per share over time and mitigates the impact of market volatility.

Earnings Per Share (EPS)

EPS measures a company's profitability per share of stock. It's a direct indicator of a company's ability to generate profit for its shareholders.

Formula: EPS =Net Income / Number of Outstanding Shares

ETF (Exchange-Traded Fund)

ETFs are investment funds that trade on stock exchanges, containing a basket of stocks, bonds, or other assets. Example: SPDR S&P 500 ETF (SPY).

Growth Stocks

Growth stocks are shares of companies expected to grow faster than the overall market, often reinvesting profits into expansion rather than paying dividends. Example: Tesla (TSLA).

Income Stocks

Companies that pay consistent dividends, providing investors with a steady income stream.

Inflation

Inflation is a general increase in the price of goods and services over time. It can also be described as a decrease in the value of a currency. Example: 2% annual inflation means prices are generally 2% higher than the previous year.

Market Order

A market order is a type of trade that executes immediately at the current market price. Example: Placing a market order to buy 10 shares of Apple (AAPL) ensures the trade is completed quickly, though the final price may vary slightly.

Mutual Fund

A mutual fund pools money from many investors to invest in a diversified portfolio of stocks, bonds, or other securities, managed by professionals.

Passive Income

Passive income refers to earnings generated with minimal active effort after initial work or investment is complete. Examples include dividends, rental income, and interest from savings.

Preferred Stocks

Definition: Preferred stocks are a type of equity that typically do not grant voting rights but offer fixed dividends and priority over common stocks in case of bankruptcy.

Price-to-Earnings (P/E) Ratio

The P/E ratio measures how much investors are willing to pay for each dollar of a company's earnings. It's a key metric for evaluating whether a stock is overvalued or undervalued.

Formula: P/E Ratio = Stock Price / Earnings Per Share

REIT (Real Estate Investment Trust)

REITs are companies that own, operate, or finance income-generating real estate, offering investors exposure to real estate markets without owning physical property. Example: Realty Income (O).

Return on Equity (ROE)

ROE measures how efficiently a company uses shareholder equity to generate profit.

Formula: ROE = Net Income / Shareholders' Equity × 100

Stock

A stock represents ownership or equity in a company. When you purchase a stock, you become a shareholder and own a small part of the company.

Stock Exchange

A stock exchange is a part of the stock market where the actual trading happens. Think of it as the "store" where stocks are bought and sold. Example: New York Stock Exchange (NYSE).

Stock Market

The stock market is a marketplace where investors buy and sell stocks and other securities. It provides a platform for companies to raise capital and for investors to trade ownership in businesses.

Stock Market Index

A stock market index is a measurement of the performance of a group of stocks. It helps investors track the overall market or specific sectors. Example: S&P 500.

Stock Ticker Symbol

A stock ticker symbol, also known as a stock symbol or ticker, is a unique combination of letters or numbers that identifies a company's publicly traded shares on a stock exchange. Example: AAPL for Apple Inc.

Value Stocks

Value stocks are shares of companies considered undervalued compared to their intrinsic worth, often identified by low P/E ratios. Example: Ford Motor Company (F).

QUIZ ANSWER KEY

Chapter 1: What is a Stock?

1. Definition: What does owning a stock represent?

A. Ownership in a company

B. A loan to a company

C. A product offered by the company

D. A company's revenue source

2. Real-World Application: If you own 100 shares of a company that issues $5 per share as a dividend, how much passive income do you earn annually?

A. $50

B. $500

C. $1,000

D. $2,000

3. Stock Ticker Symbols: Which of the following is an example of a stock ticker symbol?

A. APPL for Apple

B. KO for Coca-Cola

C. AMZ for Amazon

D. WASH for Washing Machines

Chapter 2: The Stock Market

1. Stock Exchanges: What is the key difference between the NASDAQ and NYSE?

   A. NASDAQ is physical, NYSE is electronic

   B. NASDAQ is tech-focused, NYSE has a trading floor

   C. NASDAQ is smaller than NYSE

   D. NASDAQ deals only in commodities

2. Market Function: If demand for a stock increase dramatically, what happens to its price?

   A. It decreases

   B. It remains the same

   C. It increases

   D. It depends on the stock exchange

3. Indexes: Which index tracks 500 of the largest U.S. companies?

   A. Dow Jones Industrial Average

   B. NASDAQ Composite

   C. S&P 500

   D. Russell 2000

Chapter 3: Types of Stocks and Investment Instruments

1. Stock Types: Which type of stock typically provides voting rights and variable dividends?

   A. Preferred stocks

   B. Common stocks

   C. Growth stocks

   D. Income stocks

2. ETFs: What is one key advantage of investing in an ETF?

   A. Higher dividend yields than mutual funds

   B. Ability to trade like individual stocks

   C. Guaranteed returns

   D. No management fees

3. Real-World Example: If an investor buys shares of Realty Income (O), what type of investment are they making?

   A. A mutual fund

   B. A blue-chip stock

   C. A REIT

   D. A value stock

Chapter 4: Key Financial Metrics

1. P/E Ratio: If a company's stock price is $120 and its EPS is $10, what is its P/E ratio?

   A. 12

   B. 10

   C. 20

   D. 15

2. Dividend Yield: If a company pays an annual dividend of $2 and its stock price is $40, what is its dividend yield?

   A. 2%

   B. 4%

   C. 5%

   D. 6%

3. Financial Efficiency: What does a Return on Equity (ROE) of 20% signify?

   A. The company generates $20 in revenue for every $100 of shareholder equity.

   B. The company generates $20 in profit for every $100 of shareholder equity.

   C. The company owes $20 for every $100 of shareholder equity.

   D. The company has $20 in cash reserves.

Chapter 6: How to Make Money from Stocks

1. Capital Gains: If you buy 100 shares of a stock at $50 each and sell them at $70 each, what is your total capital gain?

   A. $1,000

   B. $2,000

   C. $5,000

   D. $7,000

2. Dividends: If a company pays a dividend of $3 per share and you own 200 shares, how much annual income will you receive?

   A. $200

   B. $300

   C. $600

   D. $1,200

3. Combined Strategies: What is a potential benefit of combining capital gains and dividend income?

   A. Guaranteed returns

   B. Diversified income streams

   C. Lower tax rates

   D. Risk-free investing

Chapter 8: Risks and Considerations

1. Market Risk: What is an example of market risk?

   A. A company faces declining sales.

   B. Stock prices drop due to an economic recession.

   C. A company's CEO resigns unexpectedly.

   D. A company announces a product recall.

2. Volatility Risk: If a stock experiences frequent sharp price increases and decreases, it is considered:

   A. Stable

   B. Overvalued

   C. Volatile

   D. Undervalued

3. Diversification: How does diversification help reduce risk?

   A. It guarantees higher returns.

   B. It spreads investments across different asset types.

   C. It eliminates losses completely.

   D. It focuses investments on one industry.

Chapter 9: Getting Started

1. Risk Tolerance: What type of investor would prefer bonds and dividend-paying stocks?

   A. Conservative

   B. Aggressive

   C. Speculative

   D. Moderate

2. Brokerage Accounts: Which type of broker is best for beginners seeking low fees and educational resources?

   A. Full-service broker

   B. Online broker

   C. Robo-advisor

   D. Investment bank

3. Dollar-Cost Averaging: What is one advantage of dollar-cost averaging?

   A. It guarantees profits.

   B. It eliminates the need for diversification.

   C. It reduces the impact of market volatility.

   D. It requires less initial capital.

CONCLUSION

Congratulations on completing the Black Family Guide to Stocks! By exploring fundamental concepts, strategies, and practical tools, you now have the knowledge needed to begin your investing journey with confidence. Here are the key points to remember as you move forward:

Start Small and Stay Consistent

Determine your WHY... your reason for saving / investing. Begin with an amount you're comfortable investing in and use strategies like dollar-cost averaging to build your portfolio over time.

Diversify Your Portfolio

Spread your investments across sectors, industries, and asset types to reduce risk and maximize returns.

Keep Learning

- Use the additional resources and glossary provided to deepen your understanding of the stock market.
- Stay informed about market trends, economic news, and company performance.

Monitor and Adjust

Regularly review your investments and rebalance your portfolio to ensure it aligns with your goals and risk tolerance.

Remember, investing is a long-term journey that requires patience, discipline, and a clear strategy. By applying what you've learned in this guide, you're well on your way to building wealth and achieving financial success.

Good luck on your investing journey!

SOURCES

This book, **The Black Family Guide to Stocks: *Simple Strategies for Investing and Building Wealth,*** was developed using insights, examples, and foundational knowledge from various trusted sources in the field of investing and financial education. Below is a list of resources that informed the content:

Books and Publications

- Benjamin Graham, The Intelligent Investor: A timeless guide to value investing and risk management.
- Burton Malkiel, A Random Walk Down Wall Street: Covers key investment strategies and the importance of diversification.
- Philip Fisher, Common Stocks and Uncommon Profits: Insights on identifying high-potential growth stocks.

Websites and Educational Platforms

- Investopedia: Definitions, explanations, and real-world applications of financial metrics and stock market concepts. (www.investopedia.com)
- Morningstar: Comprehensive analysis and ratings for stocks, ETFs, and mutual funds. (www.morningstar.com)
- U.S. Securities and Exchange Commission (SEC): Access to company filings and investor education resources. (www.sec.gov)
- Yahoo Finance: Real-time data, company financials, and analysis of stock performance. (www.finance.yahoo.com)

Stock Market and Trading Tools

- Fidelity Investments: Educational tools for beginner investors and portfolio tracking.
- Robinhood: Insights into fractional investing and trading platforms.
- Vanguard: Guides on dollar-cost averaging, risk tolerance, and asset allocation.

Economic and Market Research

- Bloomberg: Analysis of stock indexes, economic factors, and corporate performance. (www.bloomberg.com)
- CNBC: Coverage of market news, trends, and investor sentiment. (www.cnbc.com)

Real-World Examples and Case Studies

- Historical data and trends from companies such as Apple (AAPL), Tesla (TSLA), Coca-Cola (KO), and Procter & Gamble (PG) were used to illustrate financial metrics and investment strategies.
- Insights into stock indexes (S&P 500, NASDAQ Composite, and Dow Jones Industrial Average) were drawn from industry data and financial reporting.

Personal Finance Education Resources

- Bankrate: Guides on dividend investing and inflation considerations. (www.bankrate.com)
- NerdWallet: Beginner-friendly explanations of investment terms and strategies. (www.nerdwallet.com)
- Real Estate Investment Trusts (REITs)

- REIT-specific data and examples, such as Realty Income (O), were informed by industry publications and REIT investor reports.

Disclaimer

The content of this book is for educational purposes only. The sources listed above were used to ensure the accuracy and relevance of the material. However, readers are encouraged to conduct their own research and seek professional advice tailored to their specific investment goals and financial situation.

www.ingramcontent.com/pod-product-compliance
Lightning Source LLC
LaVergne TN
LVHW010938110826
845149LV00013B/2650